ALABASTER

FSC
www.fsc.org
MIX
Paper | Supporting
responsible forestry
FSC® C013123

Printed in Italy by Graphicom S.p.A.

Library of Congress Cataloging-in-Publication Data is available upon request. Library of Congress Control Number: 2022913161

ISBN: 978-1-952357-44-2

Contact:
hello@alabasterco.com
www.alabasterco.com

Alabaster Co explores the intersection of creativity, beauty, and faith. Founded in 2016. Based in Los Angeles.

FRUIT

Love

Joy

Peace

Patience

Kindness

Goodness

Faithfulness

Gentleness

Self-control

8

22

38

58

76

90

104

122

138

INTRODUCTION

The sweet, seedy cocoons we call fruits are signals of nourished roots, ripened flesh, and new life. The Fruit of the Spirit contains similar meaning. It results from the Holy Spirit's dwelling with us, and us with it. It buds with our blossoming character, into maturity. And it bears within it, the seeds of a renewed reality.

From the Garden of Eden to the Age of Information, the Fruit of the Spirit blooms on all of God's story. To engage with it is to travel a terrain of delight, discipline, and destiny. It is to commune deeply with the Holy Spirit, allowing it to influence and imprint us. Paul does not describe the fruits as separate components of a cornucopia, but as a singular Fruit—one with nine shades, textures, and flavors.

What does it mean to bear this fruit today? This book is meant to refresh and refine our understanding of love, joy, peace, patience, kindness, goodness, faithfulness, gentleness, and self-control. Just as Paul juxtaposes this fruit with "acts of the flesh" (Gal. 5:19-21), there are many constant, competing constraints that dry and damper our fruit: hatred, joylessness, anxiety, selfishness, violence, distrust, apathy, and lust. As we contemplate the beauty and challenge of fruit-bearing in a barren world, we give ourselves to the Spirit's leading and life. We reject the apparent fruits of worldly trees, and choose to abide in the garden of God. We proclaim a kingdom laden with this fruit.

It is tempting to confuse the fruit of the Spirit with standards of perfection, rather than reliable features of transformation. But as Paul exhorts us, let us remember our renouncement of the world and our commitment to Christ. The journey of fruit-bearing—both in horticulture and holiness—is slow, unglamorous, and lifelong. But on it, we walk with a welcome companion and advocate: the Holy Spirit.

As we read, may we read with the Spirit, growing in awareness of how God embodies this fruit and calls us to do the same. Amen.

01 Love

INTRODUCTION

What is Love?

The great thinkers and creatives of our world have long sought to understand, define, and discover love. Love somehow simultaneously applies to food, art, animals, people, places, and ideas. We make diverse claims of love—describing a tasty dish, nostalgic film, or our partners, or our cultures. Love manifests in deep appreciation, peace, solidarity, joy, loyalty, or even the sensation of "butterflies" in one's stomach. And almost always, love occurs between people. It characterizes the aroma of a mother cooking dinner for her family, the warmth of a friend's embrace in a moment of grief, or the delightful company of those we long to be with. Love comprises a galaxy of infinite possibility, but emerges singularly from its proud architect: *God.*

"Anyone who does not love does not know God, because God is love."
– 1 John 4:8 ESV

John's simple yet weighty description of God begs the question: how can someone *be* Love? And how do we, mere moments in an infinite story, comprehend the possibility of relationship with *Love, the Person?*

"In this the love of God was made manifest among us, that God sent his only Son into the world, so that we might live through him."
– 1 John 4:9 ESV

We might begin by understanding that God loved us first. Amidst a hurting, chaotic, and fractured world, the sovereign God moves in. God does not wait for humanity to sort itself out, but rather rushes towards humanity and, compelled by love, becomes a part of it. It is this timeless miracle of incarnate love that most vividly directs us to understand Love, the Person.

When we love and receive love under the wisdom that "God is love," our own experiences of love are given depth, substance, and richness. When we witness the birth of a child, a joyful union, or a cherished meal around the table, we experience love not only as a pleasant feeling—but as an experience of God. This love changes *everything.*

THE CHIEF VIRTUE AND VESSEL

"Jesus replied: 'Love the Lord your God with all your heart and with all your soul and with all your mind.' This is the first and greatest commandment. And the second is like it: 'Love your neighbor as yourself.' All the Law and the Prophets hang on these two commandments."

In Matthew 22:37-40, love is described as the greatest commandment on which "all the Law and the Prophets hang on." In 1 Corinthians 13:13, love is considered greater than the virtues of faith and hope. In 1 Corinthians 13:1-3, love is described as more essential than the gifts of tongues, prophecy, faith, and sacrificial giving.

Every fruit of the Spirit is a good and beautiful expression of the person of God in us—yet love is elevated above the rest. Why is this? Latin priest St. Jerome, meditates on this question: "What deserves to hold the first place among the fruits of the Spirit if not love? Without love other virtues are not reckoned to be virtues. From love is born all that is good."[1]

Love is the vessel in which all of the other fruits of the Spirit are held. When we experience joy, we love to be with God and others. When we participate in peace-making, we are enacting love in our world. When we practice patience, we become a presence of *love*. When we are kind to others, we are ambassadors of *love*. When we behave with gentleness, we interact through a posture of *love*. When we exercise self-control, we more fully understand *love*.

Love binds and begets the whole fruit of the Spirit. Love is *why* the other fruits have life. In these fruits, love becomes an orientation, energy, behavior, action, incarnation, and *person*. In our pursuit of virtue, we always begin in love.

THE BELOVED COMMUNITY

God's love is realized in our everyday living through community. Love is actualized in the truth that we humans are bound together and committed to one another by an ethos of love.

On a trip to Louisville, Christian mystic and clergyman Thomas Merton shares:

"In Louisville, at the corner of Fourth and Walnut, in the center of the shopping district, I was suddenly overwhelmed with the realization that I loved all these people, that they were mine and I theirs, that we could not be alien to one another even though we were total strangers. It was like walking from a dream of separateness, of spurious self-isolation in a special world, the world of renunciation and supposed holiness."[2]

At the center of love and community is the feeling of belonging. Though the depth of our individual lives overwhelm us—even to the point that we lose sight of others—we never stop belonging to something bigger than ourselves. When we love, we return to our state of belonging. We live in mutuality with others, sharing life rather than hoarding it. We see others as they truly are, beyond our fickle assumptions. We treasure our similarities and curiously explore our differences. And we discover that we are meant to belong in loving relationship with others.

In one story in the Bible, four people recklessly break a hole in the roof of a crowded building and carry a man through, so that he might be healed by Jesus (Luke 5:17-39). In another story, a mother courageously approaches Jesus to ask for healing for her daughter—despite knowing she is not one of God's original chosen people (Matt. 15:22-29). These actions articulate love for us—approaching God on behalf of others, allowing ourselves to be filled with empathy and compassion over their desires and needs. Loving others is not promising to solve every problem or be constantly available; it is choosing to do what we can, intertwining our lives with theirs. Love is a partnership—not a project. As we bring our friends into proximity with Jesus, we take our place beside them.

LOVE AS SACRIFICE

Loving in the way God defines and models is no easy thing; at its base, it requires selflessness and sacrifice.

To love sacrificially challenges values deeply ingrained in us. A context of scarcity forces us to save our resources, avoid risk, or mind our own well-being above others. These are good things, but we limit the possibilities of love when we allow these ideas to inhibit us from caring for those outside of ourselves and our circles.

It is easy to feel that we do not have much to offer, and taking from what we have stored and may need later—resources, time, or energy—can seem risky, challenging, and even irresponsible. The act of sacrifice necessarily creates lack in our lives, which is not often pleasant.

But by creating lack in our lives, we are digging holes to be filled and shaping opportunities to receive from others and God. If we are completely self-reliant, we miss out on the joy, trustworthiness, and love of God and others.

In Luke 12, Jesus tells his disciples, "Do not be anxious about your life, what you will eat, nor about your body, what you will put on. For life is more than food, and the body more than clothing" (Luke 12:22 ESV). Jesus spoke to seemingly essential needs, inviting his disciples to consider life as more than these. In contemplation, we are also invited to consider our values in this life. We might be moved to reconsider our affinity for safety and self-reliance. We might reconsider our sense of community, purpose, and the wondrous possibilities of discomfort and dependence. In our daily and lifelong pursuits of happiness, success, and progress, how are we limiting or opening ourselves up to love?

Jesus reminds us that our Father knows what we need (Luke 12:30 ESV). And if God knows what we need, we can relinquish our anxieties over constant consumption and security. We can even take on this model for how we love and care for others, learning to comprehend what they need and helping to provide.

Jesus is the ultimate model of sacrifice; he sacrifices his status, power, comfort, reputation, and whole life. He relies on others. He invests in relationships above all else. And he gives his life for his friends. May we let this model of sacrificial love root us and guide us. Amen.

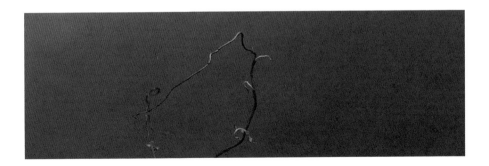

02 **Joy**

INTRODUCTION

Of all the fruit of the Spirit Paul describes, Joy is perhaps the most misunderstood. We confuse joy with general happiness—a frivolous or incongruous feeling. Through this lens, joy can seem insincere or indulgent. But this does not resemble a Biblical understanding of joy. Biblical joy is born out of the anticipation, expectation, or experience of something wonderful. It is a feeling of bliss or delight rooted in our relationship with God. In a world dominated by cynicism and outrage, joy is radical. Joy offers an alternative way to engage our lives, characterized not by despair or resignation but bursting with gratitude and hope.

God embodies and personifies joy. In the first moments of the world, God looks at all he creates—and delights in it. Zephaniah 3:17 reminds us of God's joy: "For the Lord your God is living among you. He is a mighty savior. He will take delight in you with gladness. With his love, he will calm all your fears. He will rejoice over you with joyful songs" (NLT). We have been created as a direct result of God's love for us and for all of creation. When we experience joy, we are reminded that we were loved into being; our Creator continues to provide for us and sustain us. How remarkable to be the object of our God's delight!

Luke's gospel records a song sung by Mary after she learns that she is chosen by God to carry and deliver Jesus, God's son (Luke 1:46-55). In this song, often called The Magnificat, Mary expresses that her soul has been filled with joy. Pointing to the goodness and faithfulness God has displayed in the past and anticipating the hope and glory that is to come, Mary rejoices at the opportunity to be a part of God's plan for creation. We too are a part of this plan; each day offers us the opportunity to delight in God's joyful work in all things.

JOY AS RESISTANCE

There is much that has been said on distinctions between happiness and joy. At its core, happiness is understood to be circumstantial, situational—triggered by external events. Joy, alternatively, is often described as something emerging from inside oneself—a quiet, everlasting optimism independent of circumstance.

We typically understand joy as an essential feature of a quality life. Yet when we look outwardly to the world, there is much that feels incongruent with joy. We endure loss, injustice, and cruelty. Amidst these, the call to joy might appear superficial or naïve—a fantasy incompatible with everyday living. How can one be truly joyful if they are in touch with the difficulties and sufferings experienced in the world?

Joy is not merely a reaction, but a form of *resistance*. The Merriam-Webster Dictionary defines resistance as "the power or capacity to withstand the force of effect." When we understand joy as resistance, we avoid the shallow versions of joy as avoidance, denialism, or life experienced in a vacuum. Joy as resistance involves acknowledging and facing suffering—and choosing joy regardless. Joy as resistance critiques the joy-depleting forces we contend with, inspiring us to protect and practice our joy. It is joy—not ferocity, problem-solving, or comfort—that is the very essence of resistance.

This concept runs counter to our traditional perceptions of resistance. We characterize resistance as rejection or battle, viewing the hardships of our lives as enemies we must overpower to overcome. But when rejection becomes our primary frame of resistance, we actually give our struggles power over us. We end up placing the problems we renounce at the very center of our lives.

When resistance is rooted in joy, we strip these things of their power. We allow our lives to be defined not by our suffering but by something else entirely. In joyful resistance, we recover strength from the past—and hope in what is yet to come. Suffering is a reality of our world; we cannot pretend otherwise. But when we who suffer also practice joy, we resist the all too attractive belief that there is no other way for the world to be.

The prophet Isaiah describes Jesus as "a man of sorrows and acquainted with grief" (Is. 53:3 NIV). Still, the angels of Luke's gospel describe Jesus as cause for "great joy for all people." Jesus' embodiment of grief and joy do not present a contradiction, but twin realities we too are destined to inhabit (Luke 2:10 NIV). Just as sorrow will characterize our earthly existence, joy is ours. In John 16:20-22, Jesus addresses his disciples about the suffering awaiting them. He says, "You will grieve, but your grief will turn to joy...Now is your time of grief, but I will see you again and you will rejoice, and no one will take away your joy" (NIV).

To Jesus, grief itself is the raw material of joy. We practice resistance when we face tragedy and remember still that joy is ours—our strength, our hope, and our inheritance. To practice joy is to declare that suffering is just one chapter of the story. To practice joy is to uphold a tradition of resistance embodied by many that suffered before us. And to practice joy is to find ourselves in company with Christ himself, in whom our joy is made complete.

JOY IS TO BE SHARED

Just as joyful resistance is not a denial of our current circum-stances, neither is joy a hedonistic or materialistic pursuit. He-donism is to make pleasures, desires, and comforts our primary aim of life. But to pursue our wants in this way is to be entirely self-focused and gluttonous. We witness the corrupting effects of materialism in economic disparity, the hoarding of resourc-es, and unethical consumption. These are not fruits of joy.

Embracing joy means being unified with all of creation. All of us, from the strongest adult to the smallest child, are alive and in this world because of the graciousness of God. We have hope for tomorrow not through things or promised pleasures, but because of the love God shows to us through Jesus. Joy in-volves a posture of gratitude and worship; it is joining togeth-er to give thanks to the Lord. The psalmist rejoices in Psalm 96:11-13: "Let the heavens be glad, and the earth rejoice! Let the sea and everything in it shout His praise! Let the fields and their crops burst out with joy! Let the trees of the forest sing for joy before the Lord, for He is coming!" (NLT). True joy prompts us to celebrate the successes of those around us and to uplift and support our communities. It moves us to care for each other and for our world.

Our desires are mostly shared: we all want the best for our families, good health, and security. Joy encourages us to gath-er collaboratively to share the blessings and opportunities we have been given. Worldly norms of selfishness actually rob us of joy. When we live only for ourselves, jumping from pleasure

to pleasure, our eyes become constantly fixed on what comes next. We focus primarily on what we do not yet have. Selfishness places our satisfaction and security in competition with the satisfaction of others. But, in truth, the lines of division and competition are illusions. We are united under God—all of us created in the image of God. When we are united with one another and work towards a common good, we choose joy. We see this notion reflected in the words of Psalm 106:3: "There is joy for those who deal justly with others and always do what is right" (NLT). The fullness of joy is lived out when we stand up for justice and mercy.

This joyful care extends beyond human interaction, into the way we treat the earth. We ought not view nature through the common lens of material exploitation. Instead, let us recognize that the natural resources of this planet—the soil, plants, animals, oceans, skies, and landscapes—are wonderful and vital parts of God's creation, just as we are. God delights in creation; let us rejoice in it also.

JOY AS DISCIPLINE

Once we understand what joy is, how can we be intentional about embracing it? What does it look like to cultivate and live out joy? To experience the fruit of joy as Paul describes requires us to engage joy as an ongoing, deliberate practice—a spiritual discipline.

For some, discipline may have negative associations with legalism, repression, or penalty. But at their best, spiritual disciplines are guiding gifts to help us experience joy in our daily lives. They are opportunities to commit and recommit ourselves to living mindfully. Living into and out of joy is counter to our cultural nature, which is increasingly cynical and nihilistic. It requires practice and thoughtfulness. As Paul writes in Galatians 6:7, "You will always harvest what you plant" (NLT). That which we fix our attention upon will be the first thing we see.

We are not alone in seeking the discipline of joy. The practice of joy as a discipline is well-documented throughout the history of the Christian faith. In Deuteronomy 16:14-15, enacting joy was a prescribed part of many religious festivals: "Be joyful at your festival—you, your sons and daughters, your male and female servants, and the Levites, the foreigners, the fatherless and the widows who live in your towns. For seven days celebrate the festival to the Lord your God at the place the Lord will choose. For the Lord your God will bless you in all your harvest and in all the work of your hands, and your joy will be complete" (NIV).

Likewise, David writes in Psalm 59:16, "But as for me, I will sing about your power. Each morning I will sing with joy about your unfailing love" (NLT).

Both of these scriptures demonstrate the importance of creating structures—celebratory holiday festivals or morning routines—for joy. And most vitally, they offer the heart of any meaningful discipline in joy: gratitude. For the Israelites, joy during the festivals was born out of anticipatory thankfulness for the harvest the Lord would provide. For David, joyful singing each morning is made possible by God's continual protection and guidance.

Research professor Brené Brown discusses the idea of joy as a discipline of gratitude: "I never talk about gratitude and joy separately...In 12 years, I've never interviewed a single person who would describe their lives as joyful, who would describe themselves as joyous, who was not actively practicing gratitude."[1]

Gratitude invites us to reflect and take stock of all that we have to be thankful for. Even in our lowest moments, we can be grateful to be made by a loving God in God's image. Gratitude fixes our focus on what we have been blessed with, rather than what we think we are missing. Practicing gratitude leads directly into the practice of joy. If joy is a feeling of bliss or delight born out of the anticipation of something wonderful, gratitude is what enables us to anticipate. When our focus is on the next goal or hurdle, daily opportunities to rejoice can pass us by unheeded. Instead, let us take time to pause and give thanks for what God has put before us. To reflect on and give thanks for our blessings is to root ourselves in Joy. Amen.

03 **Peace**

INTRODUCTION

We live in unstable times. Strife and chaos of many forms appear to be on the rise. Governments fall, pandemics rage, weapons of mass destruction are tested, ecosystems disintegrate, and natural disasters increase in intensity. On an interpersonal level, unkind treatment, indifference to suffering, and political sectarianism sows fear and mistrust.

While the term "unprecedented" is the flavor of our moment, this existential sense of impending chaos has been shared by many throughout history—including those living during Jesus's birth in Judea. At the time, the Israelites had endured Roman occupation for generations and unrest was building. Zealots plotted violent revolution as many common people suffered.

Amidst this tumult, the Son of God is born to an unwed teenage girl in a barn in Bethlehem. He is the fulfillment of Isaiah's prophecy of the One who will come as "Wonderful Counselor, Mighty God, Everlasting Father, and Prince of Peace" (Is. 9:6). Jesus' life and teachings challenge what people think of as the Kingdom of God. It is not one of forceful imperial takeover, but one best characterized by a mustard seed or yeast (Matt. 13:31-34). Slowly, almost imperceptibly, it grows and spreads through hearts and societies. One of the hallmarks of those who belong to this Kingdom, Paul writes in Galatians, is Peace.

DEEP-ROOTED PEACE

As Jesus prepares to leave his disciples on the night before his crucifixion, he has an intimate conversation with them about what is to come (John 13-17). He is going away, he says, but will not leave them orphaned. He is sending an Advocate, the Holy Spirit. Jesus prepares his disciples for persecution, sorrow, and pain in his absence. Even so, he promises peace.

"Peace I leave with you; my peace I give to you. I do not give to you as the world gives. Do not let your hearts be troubled, and do not let them be afraid." – John 14:27 NRSV

Like the first disciples, we who follow in Jesus' steps today have good reason to be troubled. Anxiety, stress, and worry are dominant forces in our world. Though we may not be physically persecuted, the news cycle constantly feeds the feeling that the world as we know it is coming to an end. In our families and communities too, we hear of people losing jobs and livelihoods, tragic deaths, churches splintering from conflict and abuse, and endless iterations of human suffering.

Interestingly, Jesus does not say, "Do not feel pain or sorrow." He acknowledges that the disciples will "weep and mourn" (John 16:20 NRSV). It is right to lament the hurts we witness and experience. But as we enter into the pain of the world, we must stay connected to something deeper. In John 15, Jesus' oft-quoted teaching on the vine and the branches, he reveals the source of our peace—a deep-rooted abiding in God's love. The only way to bear the fruit of peace is to abide in Christ, just as grape branches join to the main vine.

On a visit to California's wine country, writer and editor Al Hsu notes that deep-rooted grapevines can have roots that plunge up to 40 feet into the ground.[1] They can access aquifers even in the midst of drought, accessing the soil's rich minerals and nutrients and producing full-flavored grapes as a result of their struggle. Old-growth vines can also bear the best fruit after 60, 100, or even 140 years of growth.

In God's deep wisdom as manifested in the genus *vitis* (grape plants), we see that joining to the "true vine" of Christ allows us to endure the storms of anxiety, fear, and worry which threaten to pull us up from the soil of our existence. We can have peace because we live in and through Christ. On our own, we might put down shallow, easily disturbed roots. But in faith, we are grafted into Christ's everlasting relationship with God the Father and the Holy Spirit. We access an aquifer that will not dry up. Nourished by God's sustaining love, we know that we walk into a future where Christ meets us at every turn.

"There is no pit so deep that He is not deeper still," said Corrie Ten Boom's sister Betsie, as the sisters endured a Holocaust concentration camp.[2] Today, we face many pits, individually and collectively. Christ's promise is that even if we fall into them, even in the miry depths—He is with us. His spirit abides in us. Below the swirl of anxiety and stress that we will inevitably experience in this world, our hearts are kept in a peace which surpasses all understanding (Phil. 4:6).

PEACE AS THE PRESENCE OF JUSTICE

Jesus is clear that the peace he promises is not of complicity or complacency—which is the world's version of peace. It is not a preservation of the status quo.

In a statement seemingly antithetical to his words of peace in John 14, Jesus tells his disciples at the beginning of his ministry, "Do not think that I have come to bring peace to the earth; I have not come to bring peace, but a sword. For I have come to set a man against his father, and a daughter against her mother, and a daughter-in-law against her mother-in-law; and one's foes will be members of one's own household" (Matt. 10:34 NIV). We can see the truth of Jesus' words in our times. The many varying interpretations of what it means to follow Christ causes divisions in churches and families.

As followers of Christ, we cannot necessarily rely on what we have been taught by past generations. We must work out anew, with honesty and faithfulness, what it means to seek God's Kingdom and righteousness in our context. Sometimes, this seeking will put us in tension with past assumptions and social arrangements. This, too, is part of our calling to peace.

"Blessed are the peacemakers, for they will be called children of God," Jesus says in his Sermon on the Mount (Matt. 5:9 NIV). Note that Jesus blesses those who make peace, not those who keep peace. Peacemaking is an active process that involves seeking justice and righting wrongs, not preserving (or silently allowing) systems to continue that diminish the humanity and thriving potential of all people made in God's image.

The Reverend Martin Luther King Jr. further clarified this distinction. In 1963, jailed in Birmingham

after non-violently protesting for equal rights for Black Americans, he responded to calls from the white church for "unity" and "moderation." Those who issued these calls, he wrote, were "more devoted to 'order' than to 'justice'" and preferred "a negative peace which is the absence of tension to a positive peace which is the presence of justice."[3]

In other words, people who have benefited from unjust social arrangements may speak of peace when they really mean "order"—for things to stay the same. But viewed from below, from the perspective of those who have been excluded from these privileges, this is not true peace. True peace comes when those who are currently poor, hungry, weeping, and excluded (Luke 6:20-22) are welcomed as full members into God's Kingdom. These are the ones Jesus calls "blessed" and the ones we ought to learn from when we seek to bear the Spirit's fruit of peace.

GOD'S INVITATION TO SHALOM

What does this powerful, participatory, positive peace look like? Though we do not often see it lived out in our world, let us not deny its possibility. Theologian Randy Woodley writes, "The Creator has embedded this desire deep in the core of our being. The Scriptures are replete with words and images of what such a world would look like."[4] We were made for peace.

Woodley goes on to explore a Biblical vision of *shalom*, which is the Hebrew word for peace. The root meaning of shalom is wholeness, completeness, and well-being. We witness a picture of it in Isaiah's prophecies, when the nations go up to Jerusalem to learn God's ways, abandoning war and beating spears into pruning-hooks (2:3-4). In another beautiful passage, Isaiah describes how the wolf and the lamb, the calf and the lion, lie down together, and a little child leads the way. "The earth will be full of the knowledge of the Lord, as the waters cover the sea" (11:6-9 NRSV).

Peace, as God intends, is not just for individuals, but for communities, nations, and indeed, the entire earth. As Woodley explains, Isaiah's image of the predators lying down with prey would be the epitome of insecurity for pastoral communities that relied on protecting their flocks from danger to secure their livelihoods. But in God's Kingdom, we no longer need to rely on mechanisms of self-sustenance, self-preservation, and self-defense. "Warring over turf, wealth, or national security are extinct practices," Woodley writes.[5]

We operate by a different logic, because our existence is secured not by our own power, but by Christ. We do not obtain what we need by dominating those who are not in our "tribe." Instead, we find common ground in the work of Christ.

"For he is our peace; in his flesh he has made both groups into one and has broken down the dividing wall, that is, the hostility between us."
– Ephesians 2:14 NRSV

When we settle into a right relationship with God, knowing that we are God's creatures and receive all things from his hand, we are then able to live in right relationship with our neighbors and even our so-called "enemies." The fruit of peace can permeate all levels of relationships—from family interactions, to economic and political systems, to how we relate with the rest of God's creation, including the wolves, lambs, marshes, and glaciers. We no longer need to jostle for scarce resources but can receive God's abundant life (John 10:10). We belong together in the Kingdom of God.

But we are not there yet. Jesus proclaims that his Kingdom is at hand (Luke 4:21) and yet describes it as not fully arrived (Matt. 24-25). We live in the in-between, seeing glimpses of what God's incoming reign will be like. We hope and act on the promise of the Kingdom's fulfillment. In the meantime, we abide in Christ and Christ's spirit abides in us. Slowly but surely, we bear the fruit of Peace. Amen.

04 Patience

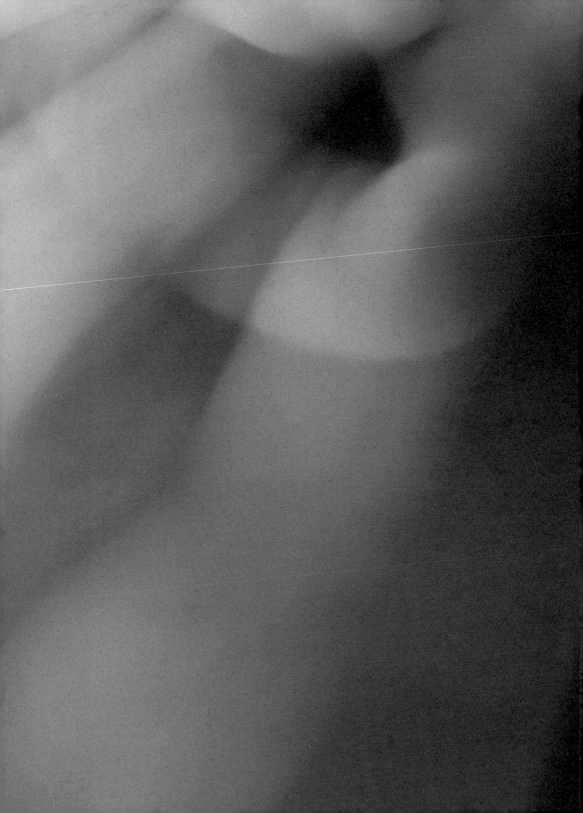

INTRODUCTION

How fast does Almighty God, Master of the Universe, move? How fast does the One who radiates light—the fastest observable phenomenon in the universe—move? About three miles an hour, the average walking speed.

"Then the man and his wife heard the sound of the Lord God as he was walking in the garden in the cool of the day, and they hid from the Lord God among the trees of the garden. But the Lord God called to the man, 'Where are you?'" – Genesis 3:8-9

Much like the other fruits of the Spirit, the noblest form of patience is found in God's relation to creation—God is exceedingly patient with us. Whenever we expect God to be the most impatient, God, "slow to anger," demonstrates long-suffering love (Ex. 34:6-7). God does not rush, coerce, or pressure us. This has been true since the beginning of creation.

After Adam and Eve's blatant disobedience, God walked in the garden, giving the two ample time to strew feeble leaves, to hide, to experience shame and guilt—necessary evils for growth and maturity. God could have rained down fire and brimstone, scattered thunder and lightning, and exposed their nakedness and wrong-doing. But instead, God moved at a shocking speed of three miles an hour.[1]

God cried out, "Where are you?" The question is ridiculous not because it reads rhetorical—Omniscient God knows where Adam and Eve hid—but because it expresses a scandalous decision: God decides to be the God bound to where humanity is. The One who can move heaven and earth decides to make home next to us. God starts where we are, not where we should be. God allows us to be broken creation in the long process of recreation and redemption. God matches our pace and ever so gently urges us to become who we will eventually be. And through it all, God is exceedingly patient with us.

If impatience occurs when plans and expectations are frustrated, then God is rarely impatient because God is rarely rushed. God operates on the order of eons, centuries, and generations. Every attempt to frustrate or delay his plans are ultimately absorbed into the grand arc: God is always in

control, and God will bring all things into fruition. Even in the smallest of lives, "he who began a good work in you will carry it on to completion until the day of Christ Jesus" (Phil 1:6 NIV).

God's exceeding and lavish patience with us instructs us about blooming in a fast-paced world, learning contentment through waiting, and exercising patient endurance in a world obsessed with control. God's slowness to anger is our source for bearing the wondrous fruit called Patience.

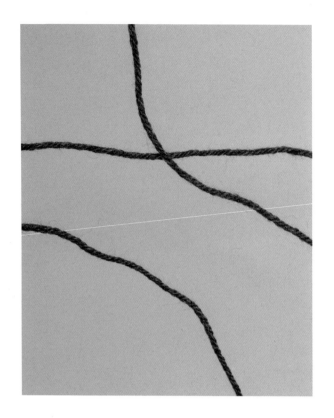

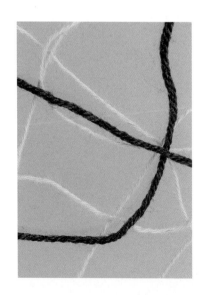

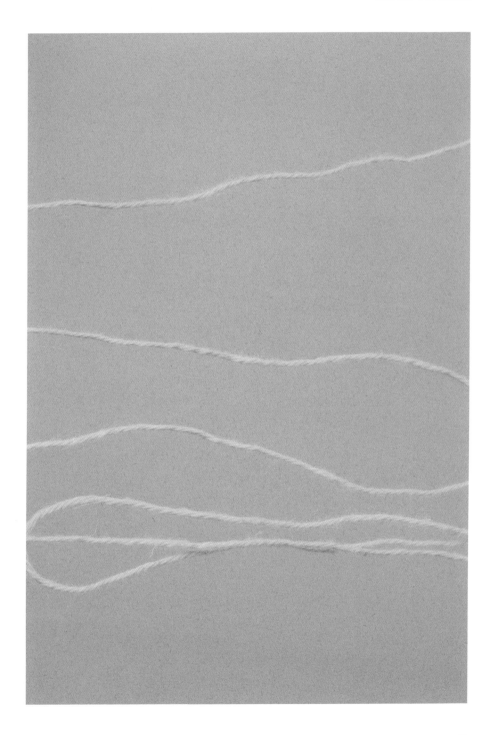

A TIME FOR EVERYTHING

"There is a time for everything, and a season for every activity under the heavens...He has made everything beautiful in its time...I know that there is nothing better for people than to be happy and to do good while they live. That each of them may eat and drink, and find satisfaction in all their toil—this is the gift of God." – Ecclesiastes 3:1, 11-13 NIV

"There is a time for everything," declares the Preacher of Ecclesiastes. Every season, activity, and feeling have their place under the heavens. Each is worthy of its allotted time, and such time is often not wasted. Time beautifies because God has made and makes "everything beautiful in its time."

But time often feels either excessive or in short supply. We feel rushed when time moves or too fast; the delivery time is too long, or the deadline too soon. Time rarely matches our liking or expectations—expectations tempered by the lust for instant gratification and the lure of productive efficacy. Instead of finding satisfaction in all our toils as the Preacher recommends, we revel only in speed: 5G, two-day or two-hour shipping, and express lanes. Traffic frustrates us, delays aggravate us, and being behind schedule annoys us as unprofessional—perhaps, even sinful. We apologize when we are late because we tend to believe that wasting another's time is paramount to stealing it.

In this hyper incubator, there is simply no time to be present. And lives that are slow, mindful, and present might be demoralized as lazy, distracted, and unmotivated. While speed and efficiency are not inherently sinful nor holy, we ought to avoid idealizing them as such. Time is not an obstacle nor mere input, but foremost a gift: every breath a grace, each season of life blessed with divine presence.

We are not masters of time, but guests of time. Our lives, experiences, and bodies are colored with the mysterious brushstrokes of time. And though beyond the confines of time, God willingly dwells within the tabernacle of time. God often selects slowness, delays, and interruptions as spaces to intervene in our busied existence.

As the Preacher of Ecclesiastes notes, time offers us a series of invitations: to bask under God's brilliance, to find satisfaction in the good fruits of our labors, and to be slow, mindful, and present. To observe how different seasons faithfully come and go, to hold dear in one's heart today's mercies and sufferings, and to feel the now-ness of life. Patience in these postures allow God to beautify us in time.

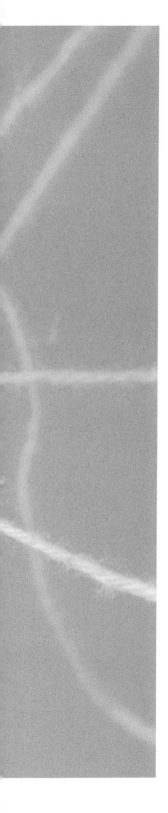

WAITING UPON THE LORD

Things take time. We are invited to wait upon the Lord.

If frenetic speed is the pace at which we so often choose to live our lives, waiting is the virtue we are continually invited into. There are seasons in our lives that feel long, arduous, and tedious. These seasons of waiting are the fiery forge where patience is brought forth and blossomed. These moments of waiting are the acknowledgement that we are far from perfect; it takes time—a lifetime, in fact—for God to beautify our lives into something complete.

Things take time. We are invited to wait upon the Lord.

It comes as no surprise when the One who operates on the order of eons, centuries, and generations leads us through seasons of waiting. We wait simply because we are time-bound. A long evening before dawn, a full season before a harvest, nine months before a birth, and, hopefully, a full life before death. Waiting is weaved into the fabric of creation.

But technological advances and modern conveniences have convinced us that waiting is inconvenient, even superfluous. Who would wait for a harvest when a supermarket has everything year-round? Waiting is not weaved into the fabric of convenience.

Waiting is yielding our time to a grander narrative. In seasons of waiting, we tender our agendas to rituals and rhythms of creation. We quell our lust for control and convenience, temptations of many technological advances, in exchange for patience. We wait with creation for the indestructible garment of new creation.

Things take time. We are invited to wait upon the Lord.

Waiting can often be uncomfortable. In waiting, we experience anxiety, worry, irritation, and resentment. Longer periods of waiting wear on us. We feel unseen, stuck, and jaded. We grow tired, our hope erodes, and the burning vision of years past flickers weakly. We become deeply discontent.

Why, then, does God bring us through long periods of waiting? Unlike waiting for a late colleague or delayed flight, this form of waiting is not idle time to be occupied with distractions, but a war where we face inner challenge again and again. When we wait upon the Lord, we reflect on ourselves, correct and love who we see, and learn to be content. We dress ourselves with truths to suppress the lies from within. We crown ourselves with love so we can lift our heads with confidence. We resemble the seasons before harvest, where we take care of the soil, absorb water regularly, and relish in the delight of the sun. In doing so, we grow in contentment during long seasons of waiting.

Growth takes time. We are invited to wait for the Lord's harvest.

PATIENT ENDURANCE

We live under the scourge of empire. Since the dawn of the Lord's resurrection—and ages before it—humanity has endured evil powers, both invisible and visible. These powers seek to dominate all space and time, personal and public. Their obsession is control. Imperial control comes in many forms: swaying appetite, hampering expectations, and corrupting one's vision of oneself. In our age, this often manifests as materialism, despair, and anxiety. The ultimate sign of imperial invasion and domination is fear—or the belief that empire is in complete control, and nothing will ever change. Writing to fearful Christians living in empire, James admonishes them with these words:

"Be patient, then, brothers and sisters, until the Lord's coming...As you know, we count as blessed those who have persevered. You have heard of Job's perseverance and have seen what the Lord finally brought about.

The Lord is full of compassion and mercy." – James 5:7, 11 NIV

For those who want justice now, being advised to be patient can sound condescending and irritating—as if they weren't patient before, or that to be patient is to be complicit. But James paints a different image of patient endurance, and he contemplates the man of perseverance, Job.

Job had everything. A successful and wealthy mogul with innumerable equities, a large family free from the burden of labor because of his many servants, and renowned character that God prided in. But an invisible and unknown adversary challenges God and undoes Job's life and his accomplishments. Raiders pillaged and made off with livestock, fire from heaven burned sheep and servants, and a mighty wind from the desert collapsed the house Job's children were feasting in. In one unimaginable moment, Job lost everything.

Nevertheless, Job immediately knelt and worshiped the Lord. While this is an extraordinary response to horrendous evils, this is not the patient endurance Apostle James had in mind. After seven days of silent mourning,

Job begins his fiery protests to God about divine justice. Why do righteous people suffer evil? Why do the wicked go unpunished? When will God respond to injustices? Job's protests stream as raging rivers, forceful in demand and eloquent in speech. But in all his protestations, Job clings to God and patiently endures divine silence. Job waits for divine response. God comes with a storm—thundering majesty, sovereignty, and wisdom. Only God can tame chaos and bring order to creation—not by might only but by divine wisdom. Job once again falls silent, not out of grief but awe. He was answered. The Lord came. The Lord is in control.

This is the patient endurance Apostle James had in mind: not complacency nor apathy, but energetic engagement with God. Patient endurance wrestles with

God—a movement involving both angry protest and close embrace. Patient endurance is bold enough to accuse God but also humble enough to receive God's rebuke and affirmations. Patient endurance firmly believes that God, not empire, is in control, and that the Lord will come again.

The Lord's coming is the full realization of the divine sovereignty and partnership with creation. The Lord will expose the great lie that evil powers and principalities are in control. The Lord will judge them not only for heinous acts against creation, but also for usurping the Lord's throne over creation. The Lord will establish God's Kingdom on earth as it is in heaven. The Lord will dwell with creation. We await, eagerly yet patiently, with all of creation for this day—the day that sets the long, dark chapter and dawns the eternal brightness. Amen.

05 **Kindness**

INTRODUCTION

God is *kind*. The scriptures are full of stories expressing the lovingkindness of God.

"Because Your lovingkindness is better than life…" – Psalm 63:3 NKJV

"So that in the ages to come He might show the surpassing riches of His grace in kindness toward us in Christ Jesus." – Ephesians 2:7 NASB

"How precious is Your lovingkindness, O God!" – Psalm 36:7 NKJV

Often, we understand the fruit of Kindness as niceness. But while niceness appears of surface-level pleasantry or agree-ableness, kindness speaks to something deeper and more precious. The original Hebrew word for kindness is often *checed*—which describes two defining attributes of kindness: favor and goodness.

Historically, favor involved provision of physical benefits to other people—especially those in need or low-positions. It manifested as giving food to the poor, caring for the sick, or sharing possessions with the underprivileged. It was defined by God showing mercy to his people in the form of favor—blessing and providing for those in times of need. Kindness, then, is not simply an adjective to describe something; kindness is action—moving, dynamic, teleological. Kindness is a virtue discovered in the active needs of our world.

Goodness speaks to the morality and soul of kindness. When we act kind, we are not just behaving in pleasurable or gratifying ways; we are sharing in the ethical life that God desires for all of humanity. To show kindness to another is redemptive and restorative. It is how *Shalom* blooms on the earth.

In both of these attributes, kindness is given a higher vision for its necessity in the world—and God abounds in it: "But You are God, Ready to pardon, Gracious and merciful, Slow to anger, Abundant in kindness" (Neh. 9:17 NKJV). Our God displays kindness—in all its expressions of favor and pervasive goodness—abundantly. We are the recipients of this gift; we need only open our hearts to it. And as it is spilled generously onto us, we might act to let it overflow to the people and world around us.

AN ORIENTATION TOWARDS KINDNESS

The root word for kindness is kin, which translates to family or being of the same relations. Kindness arises, first, by how we choose to see others. We may choose to see others as outsiders, strangers, even enemies; or we can choose as Jesus did—to see all of humanity as family, where all edges between us and another are blurred, where there are no margins, where we all belong.

Gregory Boyle, a priest and founder of gang-intervention and rehabilitation program Homeboy Industries, reflects on these ideas, saying, "Kinship–not serving the other, but being one with the other. Jesus was not 'a man for others'; he was one with them. There is a world of difference in that."[1] Choosing to be with another—even amidst polarization, prejudices, and pain—is how a journey towards kindness begins.

We find this in Jesus' simple yet punchy teaching: "So in everything, do to others what you would have them do to you, for this sums up the Law and the Prophets" (Matt. 7:12 NIV). As we orient our sight towards kinship, our daily manners and lived out expressions change. While there are many ways in which kindness becomes articulated in the world, there are three particularly noteworthy and generative practices: empathy, charity, and grace.

Empathy

"When Mary reached the place where Jesus was and saw him, she fell at his feet and said, 'Lord, if you had been here, my brother would not have died.' When Jesus saw her weeping, and the Jews who had come along with her also weeping, he was deeply moved in spirit and troubled. 'Where have you laid him?' he asked. 'Come and see, Lord,' they replied. Jesus wept." – John 11:32-35 NIV

Mary's tears cause Jesus—the Omnipotent God and Maker of the Universe—to weep. Jesus is literally moved. Jesus could have dismissed Mary's tears and quickly revived Lazarus, swiftly and effortlessly remedying the circumstance. Instead, God moves into Mary's pain and suffering. God experiences *empathy*.

Kindness is kindled when we learn to occupy the feelings and realities of others. Their hurt becomes our hurt. Their joy becomes our joy. Their hopes become our hopes. This does not mean we agree with everyone we come across, but it does mean we find the capacity, wholeheartedly, to understand their point of view and to place ourselves where they are. Jason Y. Lee, founder of Jubilee—a media company known for its central mission of empathy—describes empathy as "the act of understanding and being able to feel what someone else is feeling. The more of that muscle, that ability we have, the more we realize that we're all human."[2]

Empathy can be learned and cultivated. We begin by placing ourselves outside of ourselves, going outside of our usual circles, communities, and comfort zones. This is undoubtedly challenging, but it is also a gift. As we develop empathy, we experience a shared humanity with all people. It is this shared identity that enables our kindness.

Charity

Charity moves kindness from an idea to something physical, tangible, and tactile. There are times, of course, when charity is given a bad reputation. Acts of charity born of obligation to ego or legalism do not represent true charity, but are shallow attempts at sustaining social approval or moving through motions.

Authentic charity is as French poet and author Victor Hugo describes: "As the purse is emptied, the heart is filled."[3] When we give, truly and wholeheartedly, we are participating in something God-like. Kindness is a flow that fills our souls.

True giving is an overflow of the abundant lovingkindness first shown to us from God. Charity, then, is not just a law, checkbox, or religious obligation; charity is a beautiful expression of worship and communion with the living God. When we give to the stranger in need, we are conceiving kindness. We are choosing to see another person as Jesus would—worthy of our resources, time, and talents. Quite literally, we are choosing to find kinship in another.

Grace

We have all been hurt and wronged by other people. Pain, hurt, and misery—particularly that which is caused by those closest to us—can be the most agonizing aspects of our humanity. In these moments, we are easily enticed to move towards violence, retaliation, and vengeance. But God beckons us to take a posture of kindness enabled by the spiritual unity we enjoy with God: grace.

Grace is difficult to display to others, because we rarely offer it to ourselves. We balance buckets of guilt and shame
throughout our lives, and all the while, Jesus is intervening
to extend an abundance of grace and freedom that we are
often unprepared for. Jesus' grace is always there, and it is always sufficient. Christian author Brennan Manning reflects:
"Grace is sufficient even though we huff and puff with all our
might to try to find something or someone it cannot cover.
Grace is enough. He is enough. Jesus is enough."[4]

"Grace is unity, oneness within ourselves, oneness with
God," monk and author Thomas Merton describes.[5] Grace
is the way towards *Shalom*, wholeness. It unifies, mends, and
protects. Grace lifts us out of our shame and into the beauty of life that is all around us. We are invited to bear this
grace towards others—to forgive, to release, and to restore.
As we do, we communicate our kinship with each other and
our *Imago Dei* with God.

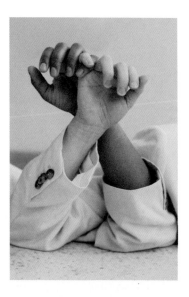

CONFRONTING THE ROOTS OF OUR UNKINDNESS

As we seek to bear the fruit of kindness, we ought to name and understand the common causes for unkindness, and reclaim them to act more generously and graciously.

Self-Interest

The primordial forces of self-interest and individuality form the roots of unkindness. Conventional economic arrangements and social identities are predicated on the notion that we must win to achieve status, success, and praise. Indeed, winning can be a good thing—competition can be fun and joyful, and ignite new possibilities of innovation and creativity. But winning must be held in tandem with the truth that winning always implies winning over someone or something else. And when left unchecked, our innate desire to win allows self-interest to fester and grow. We no longer see people as fellow humans, but rather, things to win over or tools to exploit in our pursuit for personal progress. We cannot be kind if we do not see others as kin.

Jesus' ways are starkly different from ours. In Mark 9, the disciples argue about who is the greatest amongst themselves. Jesus responds: "Whoever wants to be first must be last of all and servant of all" (Mark 9:35 NRSV). Jesus flips our competitive mindset, replacing "winner" with servant. Fundamentally, servanthood and self-interest cannot co-exist. In serving, we replace our potential for viciousness with an aptitude for sharing. Our hunger for greatness is exchanged for an appetite of generosity. In servanthood, we find our capacity to be kind.

Scarcity

It is difficult to be kind when we experience lack. Market messages tell us that we are always one step behind others. Social media feeds curate the fantasy that we are worse off than everyone else. Why should we be kind to others when everyone else has much more than us? In our society, it is easy to embrace a mindset of scarcity.

The cure offered by Jesus is abundance. In the 1987 film *Babette's Feast*, Babette, a 19th-century refugee, works in a poor Norwegian town for two pious Protestant sisters. They do not have much, and there are many reasons to assume scarcity. One day, Babette wins the lottery; instead of using the money to depart from her unpleasant situation, she decides to spend it all on cooking a lavish French meal for the poor townspeople. The sisters are moved by the meal but shocked at Babette's spending, claiming, "now you will be poor for the rest of your life." Babette famously replies: "A great artist is never poor."[6]

Babette's Feast reveals that abundance arrives from more than circumstance and physical materiality—it is rooted in things of God: soul, being, communion, and flow. Artists are often the ones who nurture us out of our scarcity mindset, to the place of abundance. To make anything beautiful requires a lens of generosity. As artists create from this place, they are imbuing kindness into the world. We must follow the artist's lead. When we take on the spirit of abundance, our petty attitudes towards others are exchanged for radical, extravagant kindness. The world becomes more beautiful.

THE RANDOM, INFECTIOUS
PRACTICE OF KINDNESS

Random

In our world, this fruit is often described as "random acts of kindness." There is something wonderfully haphazard, irregular, and random about kindness. While many of the other fruit of the Spirit require prolonged intentionality and intense deliberation, kindness seems to surprise at any moment and in the most unplanned of circumstances. Kindness is helping a senior neighbor carry her groceries up the stairs, or buying ice cream for a child. It is paying for someone's meal on a whim, or volunteering for a community project. It is planting a tree or writing a note of encouragement to a coworker.

Whether we give or receive them, we rarely forget these random acts of kindness. They cut through the monotony and routine of life, inspiring in us fresh perspective and hope. Jesus' ministry was strangely random. In a chronological sense, Jesus' travel through Judea, Samaria, and Galilee reveal an oddly inefficient and unsystematic set of movements. Jesus moved in zig-zags and circles, often returning to the same place multiple times. In short, it would have been impossible to predict where Jesus was going next—despite his stated mission. But this randomness actually added to the impact Jesus had on others. His miracles were powerful, in part, because they were non-sequential and unplanned. He was interruptible to urgent needs, and saw one person just as worthy of his time as thousands. Jesus' acts were random acts of kindness, healing, beautifying, and restoring others.

Infectious

In the 2000 film *Pay It Forward*, 11-year old boy Trevor McKinney conceives of a plan to do random favors for three individuals.[7] Instead of paying Trevor back, the individuals are encouraged to "pay it forward" by performing random favors for three additional individuals. By the end of the movie, the result is a "pay it forward" movement spanning the entire country.

Kindness is infectious. A warm compliment or generous gift from a stranger pulls us out of our self-centered stupor and compels us, in turn, to be kind. We might not notice the ripple effects of our kindness, but like many things in the Kingdom of God, it may only take one small mustard seed of empathetic action to shift the entire earth towards kindness. Do we look for these minute moments of taking out the trash for our neighbor? Of paying for a random meal for someone in need? Of volunteering in our community? Against the backdrop of kindness' infectious capacity, our random acts turn from unnoticeable to world-changing.

May we participate in these serendipitous things of God—empathy, charity, grace, generosity, servanthood—and may it move the world towards God's abounding lovingkindness. Amen.

06

Goodness

INTRODUCTION

The pursuit of Goodness has always been tightly bound to the human experience. Philosophers and cultures throughout history have sought to understand and teach goodness: Plato's love of form, Kant's categorical imperatives, and even the American dream of a nuclear family sheltered behind a white picket fence earned through hard work.

What is good? The Bible is no stranger to this question. The definition of goodness is a prominent thread throughout scripture. Over and over again, characters in the Bible are given a choice: will they take what is good in their own eyes or let God show them what goodness really is?

Biblical goodness, at its simplest, is being *like* God. As Jesus says to the Rich Young Ruler, "No one is good—except God alone" (Mark 10:18 NIV). God is the source of all goodness. We find goodness in people and things that reflect God's character—a character of beauty, justice, grace, and love. We call nature "good" because it shows us God's creativity. We call events "good" if they remind us of God's provision or sovereignty. We call people "good" when they show God's compassion, generosity, or mercy.

It follows, then, that the Holy Spirit grows the fruit of goodness in us. As we let the Spirit fill our lives, we cannot help but become more like God. How exciting it is that the source of goodness itself has given us a pathway to produce goodness ourselves!

CREATED GOOD

The first instance of goodness we find in scripture is in Genesis 1. God creates light, shores up dry land, grows crops, sets
space into motion, fills the ocean and sky, and populates the
land. "God saw that it was good." He says this six times. After
the last day of creation, however, we find a different phrase.
"God saw all that he had made, and it was very good" (Gen.
1:31 NIV).

What makes the sixth day "very good?"

Genesis portrays humanity as the pinnacle of creation. Man
and woman are made in the image of God—they get to be *like*
God. They are creations uniquely able to reflect God's character, beings to share his royal authority, princes and princesses
tasked with caring for the world. When humanity tends to the
world, creates beautiful things, and generates life, God calls
this very good. This is God's master plan for humanity. When
we see this plan actuated, we can look and call it good.

Genesis chapter two gives us a new insight into goodness, this
time in the negative. "The Lord God said, 'It is not good for
the man to be alone. I will make a helper suitable for him'"
(Gen. 2:18 NIV). Goodness is intimately tied with community
and relationships. To reign in creation as a *monarch* is not good.
Monarch derives from the Greek words *monos*, which means
"alone," and *arkhein*, which means "to rule." Instead, humanity
is the image of God *together.*

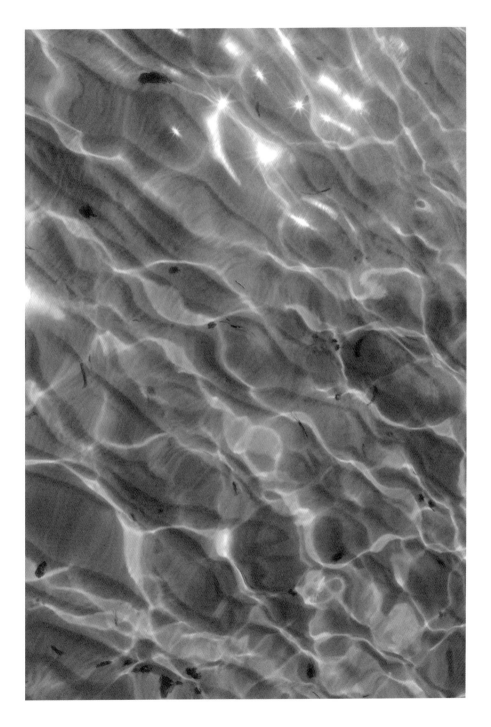

By stepping into the world of Adam and Eve, we develop a deeper sense of Biblical goodness. The garden: trees towering above our heads—each branch laden with vibrant fruit. Furry creatures chittering in the bushes—not afraid of us, simply curious. We have a divine task to care for the world around us, to develop it together. When we look at each other, we see the image of God in its fullness—its endless capacity for compassion and generosity and mercy. The air around us is filled with God's presence. Something about taking a breath makes us smile: God is with us. This is the Genesis picture of goodness. What can we call it except "very good?"

YOU WILL BE LIKE GOD?

The first two chapters of Genesis establish God as the one who defines both good and "not good." He is shown as the creator of good and the cure for lack of goodness. But, is goodness really so simple as being like God?

"For God knows that when you eat from it your eyes will be opened, and you will be like God, knowing good and evil." – Genesis 3:5 NIV

The serpent uses this very phrase, "be like God," to cause the great tragedy of Genesis. He promises divinity and goodness to Eve if she simply eats the fruit that God instructs them not to eat. Eve is given a choice. Will she let God define what is good? Or will she eat the fruit so that she can "know good and evil?" Will she take goodness into her own hands?

Ultimately, she sees that the fruit is *good* for food, *pleasing* to the eyes, and *useful* for gaining wisdom. Both Adam and Eve eat the fruit. They want to become like God on their own terms. This is the tragedy—humanity is *already* created like God. They are inherently designed as his images. They are very good. In their quest to find their own version of goodness, however, they lose the goodness that already saturates them.

We all know this experientially. Hundreds of voices in our world try to tell us what is good. A minute of scrolling through social media will give us a dozen advertisements disguised as reality, each telling us what we need for the "good life," each telling us that we can become more like God. We simply need this entertainment service or that beauty product or this piece of technology or that body type.

On a societal level, political philosophies war with each other—our minds the battleground. Each one attempts to convince us what defines goodness. If only we follow its set of ideologies, we will make the world right. Our authorities attempt to convince us that we can create a good society if we elect them into power. Like the serpent, systems, authorities, and people promise goodness. Like the tragedy of Genesis, they are sure to disappoint.

One look at the world shows us what happens when humans try to determine what is good. We see a world ravaged by war and poverty. We see families divided by past hurts and shame. We see people plagued by anxiety. Almost every person in these scenarios would say that they are trying to do good. The chronic worrier is focused on being good enough. The uncle at our family gatherings is only trying to convince us what he thinks is good for society. The armies at war—even they are fighting for what they think is good for their families, their rights, and their freedom.

Clearly, there is a *right* way to be like God and a wrong way to be like God. The journey to define good and evil feels like an unmarked path, poorly lit, with a cliff on one side and brambles on the other. We need a guide, a light—perhaps even a safety harness. Jesus offers himself as the solution.

WHO LIVES NEXT DOOR?

The first-century Israelites, just like all other cultures, debated what made a person good. They generally held that in order to make it into God's presence, one needed to fulfill the law written in their scriptures. Exactly what it meant to fulfill that law was heavily contested. In the words of one expert, the law could be summarized with these two commands: "'Love the Lord your God with all your heart and with all your soul and with all your strength and with all your mind'; and, 'Love your neighbor as yourself'" (Luke 10:27 NIV).

With such a simple answer, we might think that goodness according to the scripture should be easy. The expert in the law, however, asks a question that complicates our simple answer: "Who is my neighbor?"

Most of us have asked this before. Who is really my friend? Who am I supposed to love? This semantic question is a perfect

example of how we try to define goodness on our own terms. Looking at any people group, from political parties to cafeteria cliques, we see people trying to define who is in and who is out. As these lines are drawn, as people try to define "neighbor" for themselves, we discover more and more division.

None of us wonder if we should be good people. We wonder to whom we should be good. Our limited emotional resources force us to sift through the thousands of passersby, acquaintances, and relationships in order to allot our goodness to the people we deem most worthy of the title "neighbor." This is natural.

Jesus, however, calls us into the supernatural. In his answer to the question, "Who is my neighbor?" he does not name names nor does he assign adjectives for us to determine who qualifies. Instead, he tells The Story of the Good Samaritan, a story of a man filled with compassion, generosity, and mercy.

Jesus gives us the Good Samaritan as a caricature of his own life, an icon of goodness. Here is a picture of someone moved by compassion to become a neighbor to the hurting. We see a man give life-saving care to the destitute. We see merciful love given to one whom social norms would assign hate.

In the Kingdom of God, the concept of neighbor should always be expanding. Goodness always seeks to increase the breadth of its compassion. The definition of "neighbor" is not static—but something that develops and increases in tandem with our spiritual growth. To live within God's definition of goodness, we must always seek more people to share it with. This is the way of Jesus, who opened his circle to tax

collectors, prostitutes, and Samaritans—people who society deemed unworthy of his goodness. This is the way of God, who, in creating humanity in Genesis, longs to share goodness with everyone. In the Kingdom of God, there are no limits to whom goodness extends.

If we really pause to contemplate this, it might frighten us. It quickly exposes how far our definition of goodness is from God's. Yet at the same time, we long for this supernatural goodness: a world with everyone living like this Good Samaritan, caring holistically, giving with abandon, and breaking down social barriers. We want our society to live within this reality. We want ourselves to live within this reality.

"I make myself a leper with the lepers to gain all to Jesus Christ."
– Father Damien

In 1873, a Catholic priest known as Father Damien moved to Kalaupapa, an isolated peninsula on the Hawaiian island of Molokai.[1] Father Damien did not move so that he could spend time at the beach or enjoy the tropical weather; he moved to become a neighbor in a community that no one else wanted to associate with. The settlement in Kalaupapa was a leper colony. In the 1800s, leprosy had no cure. Contracting it was a definite, drawn-out death sentence.

Father Damien is known for dressing the ulcers of the afflicted, establishing infrastructure in the settlement, building homes for the lepers, and ensuring that his neighbors received a proper burial. He contracted the disease after eleven years. Even with his body wasting away, he continued the building projects and medical aid until he passed away in 1889.

A life like this is evidence that Jesus is capable of producing radical goodness. As we long for this goodness, Jesus empowers us to live as neighbors. He provides the love and healing we need to love and heal others. He helps us see the image of God in the people around us. Jesus is God with us. This is the Gospel picture of goodness. What can we call it except "very good?" Amen.

07

Faithfulness

INTRODUCTION

The fruit of Faith appears trivial in a world like ours. Far from our agrarian ancestors, most of us no longer pray for a good yield of crops. Technological advancements promise us answers to every question ever asked, reducing our reliance on one another. Our culture of individualism increases the locus of control within ourselves—rather than in external forces around us. In this age of information and self-reliance, we are led to ask: *is faith still necessary?*

In spite of this, the most staggering moments in recent human history have still required faith. A landmark study found that people directly affected by the devastating 2011 earthquake in Christchurch, New Zealand became significantly more religious.[1] Amidst the tragedy of the September 11th attacks on the World Trade Center, several survivors recall the intensity with which they prayed for help and rescue.

Despite the allures of our cultural progress, we will always encounter moments that require us to reach for something beyond the here and now. There are still questions that cannot be easily answered, still experiences which require reliance outside of ourselves, and still mysteries in life. In these places, *faith endures.*

"Your faithfulness continues through all generations; you established the earth, and it endures." – Psalm 119:90 NIV

All of us have moments in our lives that require *faith*. And to understand that "God is faithful" is to understand that humanity's need for faith has remained true throughout all generations, all time, and all things. The optics of faith may appear different from our agrarian forebears, but its essence remains—calling out to us as it always has and always will. We are invited then, to re-examine and discover what faith looks like today. As we do, we may encounter the great depth and beauty of God.

FAITH AND FEAR

"A furious squall came up, and the waves broke over the boat, so that it was nearly swamped. Jesus was in the stern, sleeping on a cushion. The disciples woke him and said to him, 'Teacher, don't you care if we drown?'" – Mark 4:37-38 NIV

The disciples are petrified, wrought with fear as waves, thunder, and lightning loom over them. Jesus is the opposite—confidently asleep and remarkably relaxed. He awakes only when the disciples shake him.

"He got up, rebuked the wind and said to the waves, 'Quiet! Be still!' Then the wind died down and it was completely calm. He said to his disciples, 'Why are you so afraid? Do you still have no faith?' They were terrified and asked each other, 'Who is this? Even the wind and the waves obey him!'" – Mark 4:39-41 NIV

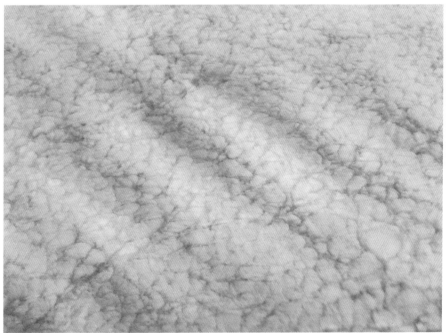

Often, we describe *doubt*—a lack of belief—as the opposite of faith. But, here, Jesus posits a more concentrated, forceful word for faith's antithesis: fear. While doubt is primarily associated with our minds, fear speaks to something far more bodily, emotional, and innate within us. Healthcare organization Northwestern Medicine finds that as we experience fear, our nervous system experiences alertness, stress hormones of cortisol and adrenaline are released, and our blood pressure and heart rate increases.[2]

Fear is something that encroaches upon our entire being. Like the disciples, we too are often mired by fear. Often, we associate fear as a common feature of many things: fear of heights, fear of loss, fear of being alone, fear of failure, fear of the unknown. Deeper, we may even fear our neighbors—perhaps not from an impending danger, but fear deriving from comparison, misunderstanding, or prejudice. In the collective, groups, tribes, and nations experience fear against other groups, tribes, and nations. Fear is an innate reality familiar to all people.

Just as we mistake doubt for fear's opposite, we mistake courage as the opposite of fear. American writer Mark Twain writes, "Courage is resistance to fear, mastery of fear, not absence of fear."[3]

Civil rights leader Rev. Dr. Martin Luther King, Jr. states, "We must build dikes of courage to hold back the flood of fear."[4] Indeed, there is great wisdom in courage. We can embrace and look to courage in hopes of overcoming fear. Yet Jesus offers another—and perhaps deeper—journey to jubilate over our terrors: the fruit of Faith.

Faith in the original Greek is *pistis*, meaning to have trust, confidence in, or fidelity. To have trust, then, is the bedrock of faith. Faith is not a call to believe in a certain doctrine harder or better than the next—it is an invitation to trust in a person: Jesus. Faith is to trust the guidance of the Holy Spirit, as it exuberates love, joy, peace, patience, kindness, goodness, gentleness, and self-control within us. Faith is a trusting relationship with the living God.

Like any relationship built on trust, faith is not a switch we can simply turn on at will, nor something we might easily triumph at. Instead, faith requires continual action, contemplation, and risk. It is a thing of dirt and grit that we must choose every day. It is a North Star we trudge daily towards, failing yet loyally continuing.

Faith is not necessarily a replacement for courage, but a foundation for it. While courage characterizes the actions we take against fear, faith is the substance that enables the possibility of courage at all. We discover courage as we place our faith, or trust, in the personhood of Jesus. Faith will take a lifetime to master, but as we embark on the journey of faith, we may find ourselves becoming more like Jesus on the boat—rested, relaxed, free of fear, and able to overcome the impending storm.

FAITH AS BELONGING TO ONE ANOTHER

The greatest extension of faith that God calls us to is the act of faithfulness towards one another. In Matthew 25:31-46, Jesus speaks of a time when he will separate the "sheep from the goats." Those who will inherit the Kingdom will do so because:

"I [The Lord] was hungry and you gave me food, I was thirsty and you gave me drink, I was a stranger and you welcomed me, I was naked and you clothed me, I was sick and you visited me, I was in prison and you came to me... 'Truly, I say to you, as you did it to one of the least of these brothers and sisters of mine, you did it to me.'"
– Matthew 25:35-36, 40 NRSV

Our choice to belong and care for our fellow humans is a direct expression of our belonging and care towards God. It is as Catholic writer Dorothy Day punctually describes: "I really only love God as much as I love the person I love the least."[5]

The practice of love inevitably requires faith. Love often becomes the vehicle of *pistis*—trust, confidence, faith—towards one another; love is a universal, embodied proclamation of our faith in God. As American theologian Robert E. Webber describes, "God works through life, through people...to communicate his healing presence in our lives."[6]

The practice of trust and faithfulness towards one another is no simple thing. In essence, it is vulnerability—exposing ourselves to the possibilities of wounding, hurting, and harm. But as social scientist Brené Brown describes, "We need to trust to be vulnerable, and we need to be vulnerable in order to build trust."[7] Trust and vulnerability go hand in hand. And it is at this intersection where we might experience the greatest expressions of life, love, and God.

As we consider how we might choose to find faith in one another, here are two noteworthy considerations.

FAITH AS LOYALTY TOWARDS ONE ANOTHER

Loyalty—the ability to display firm and constant support or allegiance to another person—is a notion often associated with faith. Yet despite its connection, loyalty can evoke mixed feelings.

As Professor John Kleinig describes: "Loyalty is usually seen as a virtue, albeit a problematic one. It is constituted centrally by perseverance in an association to which a person has become intrinsically committed as a matter of his or her identity. However, many other relationships and associations seek to encourage it as an aspect of affiliation or membership: families expect it, organizations often demand it, and countries do what they can to foster it."[8]

Indeed, corrupted conceptions of loyalty are all too common. For many, loyalty can conjure images of people pledging fealty to cruel leaders, or victims remaining in relationships with abusive partners. We need not look far to encounter the evil, exploitative, and manipulative implications of misplaced loyalty.

When practiced at its best, however, loyalty shines in its constancy; it beckons us to embody belonging and care towards one another amidst suffering, mistakes, and hardship. We are rarely eager to express loyalty in these ways. With fickle motivations, we can be quick to cut others off. And while distance might serve relationships at times, we lose out on many of God's graces when our relationships become too erratic.

Perhaps a dose of loyalty is what we need—to linger with others in trust, hope, and vulnerability, even in conflict. Loyalty highlights the capacity of faith to endure. God was and is loyal to us. Even in our faults, God continually tends to us. And as we follow God's model of tending towards others, we articulate an expression of faith persevered.

FAITH AS SOLIDARITY TOWARDS ONE ANOTHER

Solidarity is a beautiful shape of faith we share with others. Today, our lives are conveniently siloed and polarized. We no longer have to talk with those we do not agree with, nor do we have to see the sufferings of others if we refuse. But as we deepen into such chambers, we lose our sense of *Imago Dei* in the other and ourselves—that sacred, shared humanity that binds us together.

Solidarity, then, is an act of faith. To extend solidarity to someone is to put ourselves in their shoes, to trust that they might be right and we might be wrong, to nestle ourselves into their pain and suffering, and to love them wholeheartedly. While a quick prayer or act of service may suffice, solidarity often requires our time, resources, and attention. The early believers expressed solidarity by sharing "everything they had" (Acts 4:32). Such bold solidarity requires faith.

Jesus showed solidarity towards us. Amidst our hurtings, complex identities, and marginalizations, Jesus became one of us—the ultimate form of solidarity. This was not easy; he, too, required faith to live out his ministry. Our solidarity towards others is an extension of the faith embodied in the person of Jesus.

FAITH WITH

In Matthew 25:14-30, a master entrusts three servants with bags of gold. Two of the servants put their bags of gold to work, doubling the money, while the last servant chooses to hide the money away. When the master returns to settle his accounts, he describes the first two servants as faithful:

"Well done, good and faithful servant! You have been faithful with a few things; I will put you in charge of many things. Come and share your master's happiness!" – Matthew 25:21,23 NIV

But to the servant who hid his bag of gold, the man says:

"You wicked, lazy servant! So you knew that I harvest where I have not sown and gather where I have not scattered seed? Well then, you should have put my money on deposit with the bankers, so that when I returned I would have received it back with interest." – Matthew 25:26-27 NIV

Ultimately, the great mystery of faith is that it invites participation. The God who could move mountains or reshape our entire reality instead invites us to step into the universal narrative and partake within it. We literally become how God expresses faith in the world.

Consider the view of the master that the servant who hid his gold held:

"I knew that you are a hard man, harvesting where you have not sown and gathering where you have not scattered seed. So I was afraid and went out and hid your gold in the ground." – Matthew 25:24-25 NIV

Hard in the original Greek is *sklēros*, meaning harsh, stern, or violent. The servant views the master as someone to be deeply feared, to cower under—so much so that he hides away his gold, petrified. And we are not often unlike him. Rather than expressing gratitude and refining the many gifts and talents from God, we shrink away as our views of God are askew.

Christian author Skye Jethani describes in his book *With* how we live our lives *over, under, from,* and *for* God—but these are all ultimately flawed ways of experiencing him.[9] Instead, we are invited to be with God—in the mystery of communion and mutuality.

Faith is a relational journey between us and God. As God entrusts us with many things—positions, possessions, places, people—we are invited to steward them well, to nourish them, and to help them thrive. We must always bring them closer to God's intentions: good for all of humanity, on the side of joy and love, aimed towards our collective flourishing. And we must do it *with* God, understanding that the journey together will be messy, windy, up and down, backwards, forwards, and sideways. This is the fruit of Faith. Amen.

08

Gentleness

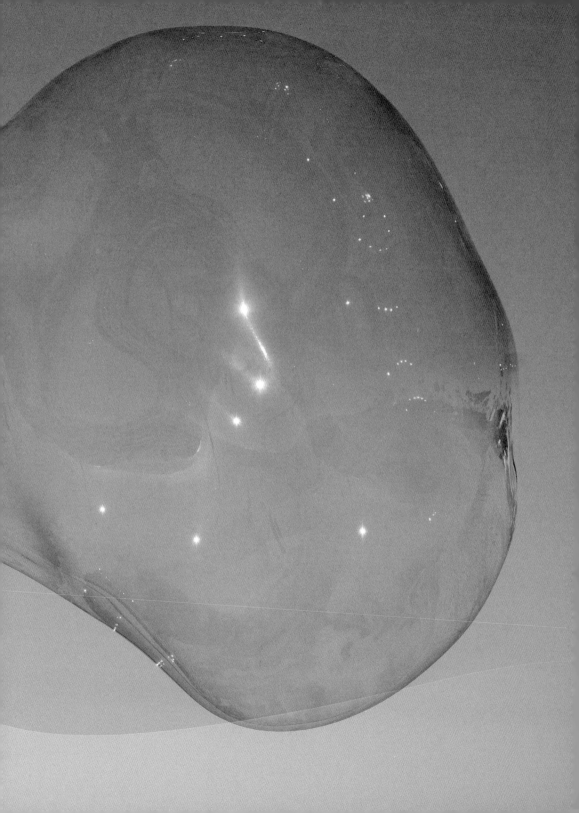

INTRODUCTION

"And after the fire came a gentle whisper." – 1 Kings 19:12 NIV

God's voice came in a gentle whisper to the prophet Elijah. Alone and in his most vulnerable of moments, when thoughts of deep failure and wishes for his own death caused him to run and hide, he was met with God as *Gentleness*. *"What are you doing here, Elijah?"* An all-knowing, all-powerful God—soft-spoken. In this dark, and cold-hard cave, Elijah experienced a shattering wind, a violent earthquake, and a consuming fire. But God was not in any of these things. God was in the gentle whisper. This reassuring tenderness, rather than heavy-handedness, restored Elijah as his despair melted away in response to the gentleness of God.

In our weakest moments of humanity, God is present with us to give the same whisper of comfort, to see us, restore, and heal. In a harsh world that can be punitive and unforgiving, God gives us permission to be gentle with ourselves as we face doubts, fears, and feelings of inadequacy. When we inevitably fail or fall, self-inflicted hostility can make bad situations worse. Cultivating a tenderness for ourselves leads us to pastures of healing, and in return, this softening gives us the capacity to be tender towards others. This is the fruit of Gentleness.

REDISCOVERING GENTLENESS

We think of an effective god to be singularly fierce, loud, and boisterous in their assertion of power. We venerate the stories of conquering heroes, and the annihilation of evil by violent upheaval of our enemies. From an early age, we like to imagine ourselves in the middle of that heroic narrative. And as we move through life, we often observe the rise of people who use domination and force to garner success—which is tempting to emulate. But strength is not a spiritual fruit. Many would rather magnify the zeal of a God that overturns tables—than the gentle hand that pulls broken people out of the dirt.

Power rooted in gentleness is rarely celebrated. But of all the fruits, gentleness might be the most powerful against evil. To receive gentleness, we must be gentle. To receive tenderness, we must be tender. Life with God keeps one's heart soft amidst a world of compression and hardening.

Among the last of Paul's list, gentleness seems to be one often discreetly set aside because of its implications. Bearing gentleness—nurturing, tender, gentle affection—is easily regarded as weak, and often by those who are loudest about their faith. Gentleness is an attribute perfectly embodied by the Godhead, but perhaps the least celebrated within our culture of intense virility.

Jesus represented gentleness in the way of paradoxes: the lion and the lamb—the lamb who suffered in silence as he made his way to the cross, and the lion who emerged on the third day. This perfect paradox gives us a glimpse of a reality in which gentleness paves the way to power, and the strong are at peace with the weak.

How do we invoke gentleness? With utter and complete humility, preferring others above ourselves, releasing our need to be "right," and pursuing the ideal of peace-making in everyday life. How do we experience gentleness? By cultivating the ground of our hearts, remaining pliable and soft; such softness is essential to our humanity and relationship with God. If we allow ourselves to become hardened, we lose touch with the part of ourselves that connects us to God and to others with empathy. We lose out on the intention for our lives in Him: to be rooted in love, and to extend grace and mercy to those who need it most.

A GENTLE TOUCH

"Just then a woman who had been subject to bleeding for twelve years came up behind him and touched the edge of his cloak. She said to herself, 'If I only touch his cloak, I will be healed.'" – Matthew 9:20-21 NIV

In a place of great need or desire, it is tempting to use and exploit others, or push and pressure our way ahead. Our culture's expression might be, "Blessed are the forceful, because they get what they want."

Alternatively, pain can make us bitter. Because of our pain, we burrow deeper into our shell, convinced we do not deserve gentleness, and neither do others. The callousness prevents the reciprocal stream of gentleness. If force is the antithesis of gentleness, callousness is its close friend.

The woman with the issue of blood had every reason to be loud, assertive, and entitled, to push and force her way to a healing Savior. After 12 years of suffering, she was desperate. And desperation can be a reckless driver. But it was her humility and gentleness in the face of her greatest need that brought her healing—gentleness, paired beautifully with self-control.

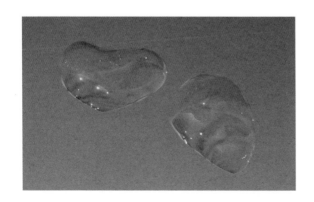

Her gentle touch broke through the multitude pressing on Jesus from every side. A gentle touch that arose above all the others because of its intent.

When Paul mentions gentleness, he uses the Greek word, *prautes*, which is of the same root as the word Jesus uses in Matthew 5 to describe those who will inherit the earth: "Blessed are the meek (*praus*)." *Praus* is challenging to translate because the English language lacks a word for gentleness expressed in power—but that is precisely what it suggests. When we allow gentleness to guide difficult scenarios, it brings with it a compounded strength and a constellation of virtues: mindfulness, forgiveness, a selfless orientation, and a deep consideration for those around you. Emotions are tempered and grounded. A kind of rest is brought forth, signifying a release of control. And hidden within this complex virtue is a promise: *Blessed are the gentle, for they will inherit the earth.* The mysterious locus of gentleness is a claim of inheritance. We do not need to furiously strive or push our way to healing, success, or power. We have an inheritance.

Meekness describes an inner condition of the heart, while gentleness guides the actions. The familiar barrage of pain, difficulty, hardship, and loss can bring a heart under siege and create a hardened shell—calloused and impenetrable. If we allow ourselves to become embittered by pain, we might

find it difficult to respond to challenges with gentleness and meekness. Gentleness might be manifested through a posture of powerlessness—which the strong so often miss. This is the upside down way of God that makes the lowly great. Our corporations, governments, and public at large all parade a brazen sense of grasping and pursuit at all costs. Meekness and gentleness are rarely rewarded openly, but are often craved by a society calloused by its own aggression. The morals of our beautiful Gospel invite us to love our enemies, care for the powerless among us, and live gently towards our neighbor and world. This can only be done by surrender, and surrender can only be done when we believe God is who He is.

"Nothing is so strong as gentleness, nothing so gentle as real strength."
– St. Francis de Sales[1]

RESTORATION OF THE WOUND

"And one of them struck the servant of the high priest and cut off his right ear. But Jesus said, 'No more of this!' And he touched his ear and healed him." – Luke 22:50-51 ESV

What love required in this moment was a gentle touch and an unquenchable heart. Without gentleness, there can be no restoration. This kind of gentleness is reminiscent of the care required for healing—a mother's touch after a scraped knee or the soothing words of a friend when we are hurt. And it is precisely this gentleness that is required to heal the deepest chasms of division between deeply polarized people. It is a special attentiveness to the injury, and a response of restorative tenderness. A surprising gentleness can heal what fury and impulsive actions have damaged. When our impulses rage, we create destruction—shouting, raging, arguing, and harsh lines drawn. When a revival of humility and gentleness comes, healing will inevitably come too.

"A bruised reed he will not break, and a smoldering wick he will not quench." – Matthew 12:20 ESV

In Matthew 12:20, we see Jesus prophetically embody extreme gentleness towards the bruised and battered. We are often broken by sorrow, sickness, anxiety, and languishing, our faith and hope hanging in delicate balance. In these fragile times, Jesus does not break us with toughness. Unlike those who prefer to be proud and trample on those already downtrodden, he is merciful and tender. This skillful tenderness is paradoxical: what is soft can make us strong. Gentleness strengthens, heals, and protects. Through gentleness, we experience restoration. In our own restoration, we are invited to extend it to others.

In the encounter at Jesus' arrest described by Luke, Jesus' presence in the garden was gentle and restorative.

Gentle enough to receive the kiss of betrayal from his friend. In the manner of the gentle voice of God to Elijah in the cave, Jesus fixated on Judas: "Would you betray the Son of Man with a kiss?" (Luke 22:48 ESV). An all-knowing, powerful Jesus—soft-spoken. Judas, in his own cave of darkness, was given this gift of gentle reflection and a chance to respond in kind—though he did not.

Gentle enough to restore the priest's servant. When Peter's response to this silent coup was to summon his sword, he delivered a deliberate and violent strike that wounded his enemy. Jesus, in response, touched the servant and healed him (Luke 22:51).

This profound moment of pause is enough to cause anyone to stop and catch their breath. Jesus was giving a firsthand glimpse at what it meant to embody gentleness in a violent world—a world that so often speaks the language of aggression to gain power. Jesus exemplifies restoration through healing tenderness. We can be sword-wielders or wound-healers, but not both. It is a spiritual act to diminish our aggressive compulsions that drive us to regrettable actions. To live gently is to create inroads for grace and restoration through the ally of forgiveness. We witness nature healing when we slow down our patterns of waste and consumption. We see inroads of impossible peace created when we quietly listen with humility and intention of understanding. Weapons are turned to plowshares. The lion lies with the lamb.

To live by the fruit of gentleness is the way of Christ. Christ embodied meekness. Meekness begets gentleness. And gentleness manifests powerful restoration—even the deepest of darkness. The power of gentleness is its endurance of the most unpleasant injuries without resentment and hardening. And even more so, it is the ability to radiate power and restoration in a deeply countercultural way.

The Kingdom of God is governed with gentleness. God meant for gentleness to be one of the nine core ways through which the Kingdom of God would arrive here on earth. Not through violence, or blunt force, or the whirlwind—but through admission and willful surrender.

The beautiful and powerful thing about fruit-bearing is that it is not just for ourselves—it is for others. In nature, the plant that flowers and bears fruit produces seed for replication. Careful gardeners choose only healthy plants for seed propagation. They select the most robust—the ones with the most beautiful flowers—which means that the good and healthy plant will multiply. When we bear gentleness, it reproduces more of its kind. Humility is a related virtue, an antidote that removes us from the center of the narrative and puts the 'other' there instead. Deriving from the word *humus* (earth), humility is a reminder that we are mixed with dirt and deity—creatures who boast of our strengths, but are inevitably fragile. Things that are easily broken require the utmost care, and gentleness is the balm for everything that breaks us.

Gentleness is the deep breath in the middle of a storm. It is a place of safety. It is the gentle current of water moving around your feet—one with enough persistence to carve canyons out of mountains. The softest whisper. The lightest touch. The subtlest movement. And unimaginable power and complete restoration through its tender fruit. Amen.

"'Not by might nor by power, but by my Spirit,' says the Lord of hosts."
– Zechariah 4:6 NIV

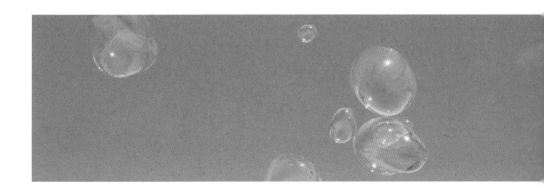

09

Self-control

INTRODUCTION

Self-control presents differently across situations. It can keep us from so-called "negative" emotions and behavior, like falling to temptation or acting rashly and destructively. But for many, the relationship with self-control is not always a good one. Some have been taught that self-control is equivalent to self-suppression, a constant insecurity, or a shameful finger-wagging into submission. Other times, the challenge of self-control may simply appear impossible. When we look to Jesus as our example, we realize that the "gold standard" of self-control is higher than we could ever possibly achieve.

Jesus' ministry begins and ends with self-control. At the start of his ministry, Jesus was led by the Spirit into the wilderness and tempted by the devil for 40 days. The devil appealed to Jesus' physical hunger, power, and pride, but Jesus—firm in his convictions—withstood the temptations. And in the last moments leading to his arrest and death, Jesus says, "Not my will but Yours be done," offering the ultimate submission of self (Luke 22:42). With such a lofty model, it is no wonder that we typically conceive of self-control as unattainable.

But if the self-control that brought Jesus to the cross was also the self-control that overturned tables in the temple, perhaps self-control is a vaster mystery than we originally assumed. Perhaps, we ought to redefine the fruit of Self-control—one that sets us free rather than restricts us, one that does not strip us of God-given emotions nor shame us into compliance, and one that ultimately relies on the Spirit and not ourselves at all.

BOUNDARIES THAT SET US FREE

To desire freedom is not to say that anything goes. Our lives should, indeed, be shaped by God's moral guidelines. However, salvation is a gift of God's restorative love and grace—not something we earn. We exercise self-control not to be rewarded with salvation, but because salvation transforms us. Self-control does not shackle us with handcuffs, for God has already set us free. This understanding shifts how we think of verses like this:

"Enter through the narrow gate; for the gate is wide and the road is easy that leads to destruction, and there are many who take it. For the gate is narrow and the road is hard that leads to life, and there are few who find it."
– Matthew 7:13-14 NRSV

God's commands are not obstacles that make the road hard and the gate narrow; they are boundaries that keep us safe and secure on the chaotic journey of life. They are like the guardrails along a windy one-lane cliffside road, bumpers of a bowling lane, or side rails of a toddler's first "big-kid" bed. They are there for our thriving. Too often, we get fixated on the forbidden and forget the freedom. In the Garden of Eden, Adam and Eve had everything available for them except the fruit of one tree.

"You may freely eat of every tree of the garden but of the tree of the knowledge of good and evil you shall not eat, [for in the day that you eat of it you shall die.]" – Genesis 2:16-17 NRSV

The serpent deceived Eve by shifting her focus from all the trees of the garden to just one forbidden tree. Adam and Eve lost focus of God's gift of an entire paradise—what they had—because of what they could not have.

When our minds focus only on the forbidden, we become re-sentful of the God who says, "Of this tree you shall not eat," and forget the God who gave us freedom to eat of all the other trees of the garden. And the boundaries in place to help us thrive begin to feel like the suffocating bars of a prison cell. However, it is God who sets us free for abundant living.

In the book of Exodus, God liberates the Israelites from slavery under the Egyptians. Shortly after, God gives Israel the Law. Were the Israelites freed only to be enslaved by God? No, on the contrary God introduces the Ten Commandments saying, "I am the Lord your God, who brought you out of the land of Egypt, out of the house of slavery" (Deut. 5:6 ESV). Under God's rule of freedom, Israel's existence is fundamentally dif-ferent than that in the "house of slavery." The Law creates the boundaries of a God-centered society that protects community relationships, gives rest, peace, justice, and order, and provides for the marginalized and oppressed.

God liberated the Israelites from the bondage of slavery and us from the bondage of sin that we might be free. The boundaries God imparts are not to hold us back, but to propel us into the freedom and abundance of a life lived under God.

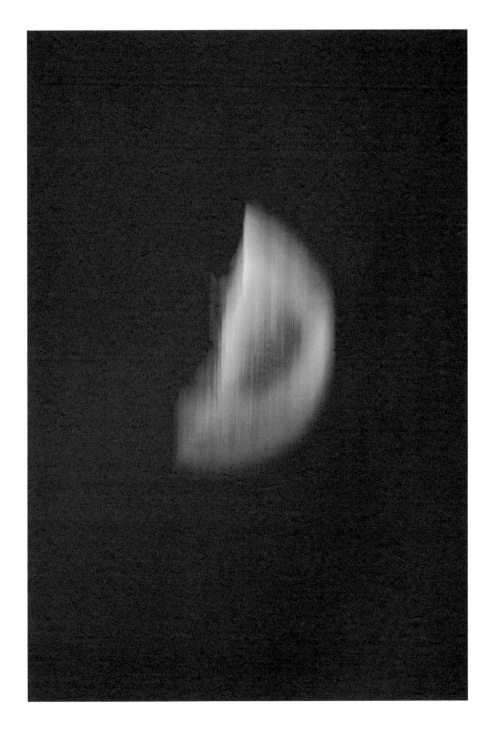

THE EVERYDAY PRACTICE OF SELF-CONTROL

In our world today, we witness the harms of no self-control: outbursts of rage and hostility, acts of violence, corruption in institutions, irresponsible and polarizing rhetoric, lapses in judgment that lead to regret, and so on.

In the Bible, Moses' lack of self-control results in premeditated murder. David's lack of self-control caused him to rape Bath-sheba and kill Uriah. Peter's lack of self-control led him to deny Jesus, not once, but three times. How is it that these beloved Bible characters fell so far from self-control as to bring about violence, rape, and death—and how is it that Jesus' steadfast self-control brought him to the cross for our salvation?

Just as Peter insisted that he would not deny Jesus, few of us plan to lose self-control under pressure. Of course, the challenge of self-control is choosing it when the stakes are high. When we face split-second decisions or enticing alternatives, the tug-of-war between self-control and licentiousness becomes an internal battle—one easy to lose if we have not prepared to abide.

In those moments, the common refrain, "What would Jesus do?" may be insufficient in prompting us into action. How do we expect to be self-controlled when it matters most if we fail to practice it when it matters least?

To this end, Dallas Willard wrote in The Spirit of the Disci-plines, "A successful performance at a moment of crisis rests largely and essentially upon the depths of a self wisely and rig-

orously prepared in the totality of its being—mind and body...
To live as Christ lived is to live as he did all his life."[1]

Self-control is an exercise of integrity that must be cultivated
in our everyday rhythms—particularly when the stakes are low
and no one is watching. It is an honest invitation for God to
examine our proclivities, desires, and motivations.

In his alone-time, Jesus rests, prays, and practices self-control.
Jesus' resistance to temptation in the wilderness, when no one
else is watching, demonstrates his integrity. When the devil
tempts Jesus, what does Jesus have to prove? No one is around
to see how Jesus will act or react. Jesus could have fallen into
temptation and no human would know. Instead, he resists
temptation and abides by Scripture, which he recites. Jesus is
consistent and integrous in public and in private.

Practicing self-control with seemingly trivial situations during
the good days prepares us to be self-controlled during the bad
days, so that when it "matters most," we can follow through. It
is in the everyday mundane abiding that our integrity is built to
be able to weather the storms and stand the test of time.

SELF-CONTROL THAT EMPOWERS

From the wilderness to his last breath, Jesus is the exemplar of a life lived with self-control. Yet, all four gospels tell the story of Jesus overturning tables and driving people and animals out of the temple. What are we to do with this account? How do we factor this into our understanding of self-control?

Some of us have been taught that self-control always occurs as self-suppression, but that is not all there is to self-control. Knowing when and how to act is also self-control. While some situations might require us to tone down, other situations need for us to amp up.

James 1:19 is often used to promote self-control: "Be quick to listen, slow to speak, and slow to anger." However, being quick to listen, slow to speak, and slow to get angry does not mean that we should never speak, never get angry, and never act in response. Ephesians 4:26 states, "Be angry but do not sin." What do we do with such anger and other emotions we feel?

In the account of Jesus overturning tables in the temple, the temple—meant originally as a house of prayer—was made into a "den of robbers," a marketplace where greedy sellers and money changers exploited the poor and the travelers. While we might read this story as a violent one—of a rageful Jesus armed with a whip and exacting judgment on the money changers—early church traditions interpreted this account as being robust but physically non-violent. Yes, Jesus overturned tables and poured out money, but he did not act violently towards the people nor did he harm the animals, as Jesus instructed the doves to be carried out and the bundle of cords he made could be used to move livestock without touching them.

Jesus' self-control empowered him to call out wrongs, disrupt exploitative systems, and make a scene—all without sinning or falling prey to rash behavior. The appropriate response to injustice is to lament, to be angry, and to do something—not to suppress feelings, remain complicit, and perpetuate wrongs.

Self-control presents differently in each situation. At times, it keeps us from temptation or tempers our so-called "negative" emotions. Other times, it calls us to righteous action in the face of injustice. The question of what expression of self-control to utilize in any given situation is ultimately not up to our "self" at all. Self-control is primarily our decision to live a life filled with and led by the Spirit toward God's will.

"If we live by the Spirit, let us also be guided by the Spirit."
– Galatians 5:25 NRSV

Jesus in the wilderness was not just a practice of self-deprivation, but rather a process of following the Spirit. Jesus' steadfastness in resisting the devil's temptations was a result of his choosing God above all else. Jesus praying, "Not my will but Yours be done," was more than just a denial of self, but a submission into God's good and perfect will.

Romans 5:8 reassures us that "while we were still sinners, Christ died for us." Self-control is not a prerequisite to salvation, but a result of salvation's transforming power towards abundant living. Even then, we must invite the Spirit into our mundane everyday rhythms, so that we might build a firm foundation of self-control to weather the harshest of adversities. Self-control is not just what we do not do, but what we do. It is to calm down or to be fired up—but it is always choosing to be Spirit-led.

Self-control completes the fruit of the Holy Spirit, perhaps, because it is required for practicing any of the preceding virtues. Only through self-control sustained by the Spirit can we blossom in love, joy, peace, patience, kindness, goodness, faithfulness, and gentleness. Indeed, the last fruit brings us back to the first one—and the ones after it. It is an invitation.

We cannot perfectly resemble every fruit, but by the Spirit, we are called to pursue, practice, and put on these things daily. And in the slow growth of seed, sprout, flower, fruit and seed again, we partake in the wonderful cycle of fruit-bearing. This is how it is intended to be.

May we live and walk by the Spirit, and bear its fruit. Amen.

 ALABASTER

SAMUEL HAN
Art Director

DANIEL SUNKARI
Editor-in-Chief & Head of Writing

TYLER ZAK
Product & Branding Director

YOOJIN SEOL
Cover Image

GRACE SUSILO
Layout Design

HALEY BLACK
Content Editor

BRYAN YE-CHUNG
Co-Founder & Creative Director

BRIAN CHUNG
Co-Founder & Managing Director

WILLA JIN
Finance & Talent Director

EMALY HUNTER
Operations & Customer Experience Director

EMMA TWEITMANN
Marketing Associate

WRITERS
Alana Freitas (Ch. 1)
Bryan Ye-Chung (Ch. 5 & 7)
Christy Chia (Ch. 9)
Daniel Sunkari (all)
Emma Tweitmann (Ch. 2)
Evie Shaffer (Ch. 8)
Kayla Craig (Ch. 5)
Liuan Huska (Ch. 3)
Matthew Hayashida (Ch. 6)
Sooho Lee (Ch. 4)

PHOTOGRAPHERS
Anna Letson
Anna Velichko
Echo Yun Chen
Jonathan Knepper
Jordanne Hamilton
Mac Elliott
Mike Sunu
Nathan van de Graaf
Samuel Han
Sophia Hsin
Tabitha Lawless
Tirza Hartono

MODELS
Amelia Lee
Angélica Herrera
Irina Erickson
Mariah St. Jean

SPECIAL THANKS
Minzi Bae – Styling (Ch. 5)
Renee Chang – Art Direction (Ch. 3)
The Loved Co. – Floral design (Ch. 1)
Yoojin Seol – Illustrator

...ne, Unknown.

...on, Lori. "Thomas Merton's Mystical Vision in Louisville." *Spiritual Travels*.
...//www.spiritualtravels.info/spiritual-sites-around-the-world/north-america/
...tucky-a-thomas-merton-tour/thomas-mertons-mystical-vision-in-louisville/.

JOY

Brown, Brené. *The Gifts of Imperfect Parenting: Raising Children With Courage, Compassion, and Connection*. Louisville, CO: Sounds True, 2013.

3 | PEACE

1. Adapted with permission from Al Hsu, reflection posted on Facebook, August 20, 2021, https://www.facebook.com/albertyhsu/posts/10157779376966256.
2. Ten Boom, Corrie. *The Hiding Place*. (Grand Rapids, MI: Chosen Books, 2006), 227.
3. King Jr., Martin Luther. "Letter from the Birmingham Jail." *In Why We Can't Wait*, ed. Martin Luther King, Jr. (1963), 77-100. https://kinginstitute.stanford.edu/sites/mlk/files/letterfrombirmingham_wwcw_0.pdf.
4. Woodley, Randy. *Shalom and the Community of Creation: An Indigenous Vision*. (Grand Rapids, MI: Eerdmans, 2012), 11.
5. *ibid*, 13.

4 | PATIENCE

1. Koyama, Kosuke. *Three Mile an Hour God*. London: SCM Press, 2015.

5 | KINDNESS

1. Boyle, Gregory. *Tattoos on the Heart: The Power of Boundless Compassion*. Free Press, 2010.
2. Heo, Yejin. "Jubilee media's founder Jason Y. Lee on cultivating an empathetic world." Los Angeles Times: High School Insider. 7 March 2021. https://highschool.latimes.com/northwood-high-school/jubilee-medias-founder-jason-y-lee-on-cultivating-an-empathetic-world/.
3. Hugo, Victor. Unkown.
4. Manning, Brennan and John Blase. *All is Grace: A Ragamuffin Memoir*. David C. Cook, 2011.
5. Merton, Thomas. Unknown.
6. Axel, Grabriel, director. Babette's Feast. A-S Panorama Film International, 1987.
7. Leder, Mimi, director. *Pay It Forward*. Warner Bros., 2000.

6 | GOODNESS

1. Farrow, John. *Damien the Leper: A Life of Magnificent Courage, Devotion, and Spirit*. New York: Doubleday, 1998.

...LNESS

...hris G. and Joseph Bulbia. "Faith after an Earthquake: A Longitudinal ...f Religion and Perceived Health before and after the 2011 Christchurch New ...and Earthquake." PLoS ONE, 5 December 2012. https://doi.org/10.1371/ ...rnal.pone.0049648.

...5 Things You Never Knew About Fear." Northwestern Medicine, October 2020. https://www.nm.org/healthbeat/healthy-tips/emotional-health/5-things-you-never-knew-about-fear

5. Twain, Mark. "Pudd'nhead Wilson's Calendar for 1894." New York: The Century Company, 1893.

4. King Jr., Martin Luther. *A Gift of Love: Sermons from Strength to Love and Other Preachings*. Beacon Press, 2012.

5. Cavadini, Catherine. "Opening the Word: Dorothy Day and exploring the gift of God's unmeasured love." Our Sunday Visitor. 14 February 2022. https://www.osvnews.com/2022/02/14/dorothy-day-and-exploring-the-gift-of-gods-unmeasured-love/.

6. Robert E. Webber.

7. Brown, Brené. *SuperSoul Sessions: The Anatomy of Trust*. 1 November 2015. https://brenebrown.com/videos/anatomy-trust-video/.

8. Kleinig, John. "Loyalty." The Stanford Encyclopedia of Philosophy (Summer 2022 Edition), Edward N. Zalta (ed.). https://plato.stanford.edu/archives/sum2022/entries/loyalty/.

9. Jethani, Skye. *With: Reimagining the Way You Relate to God*. Thomas Nelson, 2011.

8 | GENTLENESS

1. St. Francis de Sales, Unknown.

9 | SELF-CONTROL

1. Willard, Dallas. *The Spirit of the Disciplines: Understanding How God Changes Lives.* Kindle Edition. (HarperOne, 1999), 4-5.

WWW.ALABASTERCO.COM